focus on
US NATIONAL PARKS

◆ *inspiring places, beautiful spaces* ◆

Written by Donna Dailey
Designed by Jeremy Tilston of The Oak Studio Limited
Produced by AA Publishing
Text © Automobile Association Developments Limited 2007
For details of photograph copyrights see page 96

Published by AA Publishing (a trading name of Automobile
Association Developments Limited, whose registered office
is Fanum House, Basing View, Basingstoke, Hampshire
RG21 4EA; registered number 1878835).

A03202

ISBN-10: 0-7495-5209-3
ISBN-13: 978-0-7495-5209-1

A CIP catalogue record for this book is available
from the British Library.

Colour reproduction by KDP, Kingsclere, England
Printed in China by C&C Offset Printing

PICTURES FROM TOP TO BOTTOM:
The snow-dusted winter beauty of mountains and pines is
reflected in an icy lake in California's Yosemite National Park.

A shy black bear cub ambles through a wilderness marsh in
search of food. Its mother won't be far away.

Capitol Reef is one of several parks in Utah that has the fiery
orange and pink rock formations of the American Southwest.

PAGE 3: At Yavapai Point on the Village Loop trail, the sun
illuminates the peaks along the Grand Canyon's South Rim.

PAGE 4: Yellowstone's most famous geyser, Old Faithful, erupts
approximately every 91 minutes.

focus on US NATIONAL PARKS

◆ *inspiring places, beautiful spaces* ◆

INTRODUCTION

"This grand show is eternal. It is always sunrise somewhere; the dew is never all dried at once; a shower is forever falling; vapor ever rising...each in its turn, as the round earth rolls." So observed John Muir, the naturalist, writer, and conservationist who fought to protect America's wild lands. Today the system of national parks he helped to create stretches from shore to shore, preserving nature's grand show for future generations.

Native Americans were the first guardians of the land, taking only what they needed to survive and living in harmony with nature. For their descendants, mountains, canyons, and other features of the landscape are the spiritual connections with their ancestors, stretching back to ancient times. Many parks and monuments in the West are located on tribal lands.

In the early 1800s, explorers and mountain men returned with tall tales of giant redwood trees, bubbling mud lakes, spouting plumes of boiling water, bottomless chasms, and fiery deserts. As waves of pioneers followed them across the continent, their initial wonder at nature turned into a determination to conquer it. The vast grasslands of the plains were grazed and plowed, ancient forests were felled, mighty rivers were dammed, and wildlife was hunted almost to extinction. The American bison, or buffalo, a symbol of the country's great bounty, once thundered across the Great Plains in their millions. Within 30 years, they had been slaughtered to make way for the "iron horse," and their numbers had been reduced to just one herd with a few dozen animals in Yellowstone.

By the end of the nineteenth century, much of America's natural resources were in danger of disappearing forever. Fortunately, a handful of visionaries saw the inherent value of the rapidly shrinking wilderness. The fascinating geothermal features of Yellowstone in northern Wyoming led to its designation as the first national park in 1872. Meanwhile, in California, John Muir was exploring the Sierra Nevada and campaigning for its protection. "Everybody needs beauty as well as bread - places to play in and pray in, where nature may heal and give strength to body and soul," he wrote. Yosemite, Kings Canyon, and Sequoia became national parks in 1890. In 1892, Muir co-founded the Sierra Club and served as its president until his death in 1914. As America's oldest, largest, and most influential grassroots environmental organization, the Sierra Club has helped establish many new national parks and wilderness preservation systems.

Muir inspired one of the nation's most important preservationists, President Theodore Roosevelt, by inviting him to Yellowstone and taking him camping. Roosevelt had already learned the value of conservation during a brief spell as a rancher in North Dakota, and he championed America's remaining wilderness. "There can be no greater issue than that of conservation in this country," he proclaimed. During his tenure (1901-1909), some 230 million acres were placed under permanent protection. These included 150 national forests, 55 federal bird and game preserves, 5 national parks, and 18 national monuments, including the Grand Canyon, many of which have now been granted national park status.

Roosevelt was greatly supported in his conservation efforts by Gifford Pinchot, a trained forester who believed that natural resources must be managed to prevent their exploitation and depletion by private developers. In 1905, Roosevelt appointed him head of the newly created US Forest Service, which began a new era of modern land management. Later presidents followed in Roosevelt's footsteps, and in 1994, President Bill Clinton signed the bill making Saguaros National Monument in Tucson the country's 52nd national park. Two years later, he designated 1.9 million acres in southern Utah as the Grand Staircase-Escalante National Monument. In 2006, President George Bush designated 140,000 square miles of the Hawaiian Islands as a US National Monument, making it the largest marine sanctuary in the world.

Today the national park system includes 388 areas, in every state except Delaware. It encompasses not only the famous geysers of Yellowstone or the vistas of the Grand Canyon, but also scenic lakes, seashores, rivers, caves, volcanoes, monuments, historical sites, and a host of wildlife and natural wonders, from the monumental to the miniscule. The parks are places for escape and tranquility, extreme sports and relaxation. They are the last vestiges of wilderness in a country that has been tamed from shore to shore. In a land where private property is sacred, the national parks are owned by all. They are a treasure beyond monetary value, our natural and spiritual wealth.

Mount Moran is one of a dozen peaks in the Grand Tetons which are more than 12,000 feet high.
It overlooks one of the park's tranquil morainal lakes strung along the base of the range.
Opposite: this idyllic fall scene in Yosemite perfectly illustrates the words of Henry David Thoreau:
"In wildness is the preservation of the world."
Pages 6–7: snow lies like powdered sugar on the tops of the "hoodoos" in Bryce Canyon Amphitheater.
Ebenezer Bryce, who farmed here in the 1870s, called it "a hell of a place to lose a cow."

It's one very steep mile down to the bottom of the Grand Canyon, but you don't have to walk if you don't want to. Sturdy, four-legged transport is pricey but much in demand.
Opposite: the vast expanse of Utah's rugged Canyonlands National Park stretches over 527 square miles of the region known as the Colorado Plateau. Scenes from the movie Thelma and Louise were filmed here.

An airboat is a fast and fun way to explore a large area of the Everglades, which covers much of the southern tip of Florida. This enormous, grassy swamp is rich in bird and wildlife.

The red dunes of Death Valley resemble a sunburned sunbather, but there is no water here for miles around. It is the hottest, driest place in North America, with summer temperatures exceeding 120° F.

A young raccoon, looking like a furtive bandit, peeks out of a hollow tree. The Dakota-Sioux called them weekah tegalega, which means "magic one with painted face."
Opposite: the road ahead is swallowed up by the Navajo sandstone cliffs. These pinkish-beige rock formations, reaching 2,200 feet high, are a prominent feature of Zion National Park.

The red sandstone monoliths of Arizona's Monument Valley served as the backdrop to many of the old Westerns of filmmaker John Ford. They stand on reservation land and are part of the Navajo Tribal Park. Opposite: these giant sequoia trees in California's Sequoia National Park are the largest living things on Earth. They are between 2,300 and 2,700 years old and reach heights of nearly 300 feet.

Historic Route 66 once stretched 2,448 miles from Chicago to Santa Monica in California. Here, a traveler crosses the Arizona desert en route to the Grand Canyon. Opposite: when spring arrives, the run-off from snow melt in the mountains streams down the slopes, often creating thunderous waterfalls, such as Vernal Falls in Yosemite. Pages 18–19: Antelope Canyon, a magnificent slot canyon, or narrows, in Arizona, becomes a work of art when a shaft of sunlight brings out the textures and graduated colors of the curved rock walls.

21

With their shifting patterns shaped by the wind, the sand dunes of Death Valley look starkly beautiful against their mountain backdrop. It was a treacherous crossing for pioneers during the Gold Rush.

Earth and sky are reflected in the pristine waters of America's national parks. Here in this untrammeled wilderness, nature thrives and man is just a lowly visitor.

Called the "King of Birds," the golden eagle lives in remote regions where it can soar above wide, open spaces in search of prey. If humans move into its territory, the golden eagle will leave. Opposite: the Rim Trail follows 16 miles of the South Rim of the Grand Canyon. Look-out points along the way offer close-up views of the outcrops, and vistas that stretch for miles. Pages 24–25: waves of red-hot molten lava tumble into the sea in Hawaii's Volcanoes National Park, forming a completely new coastline and adding to the acreage of Big Island.

Paiute tribal lore says that the hoodoos, or spires, of Bryce Canyon were formed when the ancient Legend people so angered the powerful Coyote that he turned them into stone.
Opposite: California's Inyo National Forest has forests and grasslands which cover an area the size of Texas. These environments provide shelter and sustenance for countless wild species which would not otherwise survive in our modern world.
Pages 28–29: thanks to the preservation efforts of John Muir (who was the co-founder of the Sierra Club), as well as other campaigners, Yosemite Valley today looks much the same as when Muir arrived in 1868.

For outsiders, the Everglades present a fascinating but unfamiliar environment, with plants and animals found nowhere else in the country. Boardwalks provide a safe view of swamp crocodiles basking in the sun.

Centuries of erosion by wind, water, ice, and snow have carved out amazing shapes in the red-rock giants of Arches National Park. Here, the North Window looks out on this surreal desert landscape.

The forests of dry mountain ranges, such as the Rockies, are home to shy predators. A lucky photographer
spied this bobcat on a branch, awaiting the moment to pounce on its prey.
Opposite: Delicate Arch, which spans 33 feet and is 45 feet tall, is one of the many natural wonders in
Arches National Park in Utah.
Pages 34–35: the Everglades are a unique environment. More than 40 mammal species, 350 bird varieties,
500 kinds of fish, and 50 other types of reptile give a hungry alligator reason to smile.

From dry desert to alpine tundra, thousands of plant varieties flourish in the micro-climates of the national parks. Here in Yosemite, woodland wildflowers herald the spring.

Opposite: the sandstone rock formations of the Southwest are spectacular to gaze upon, but nothing beats the thrill of walking among them. Hiking trails in the parks give access to this majestic landscape.

Pages 38–39: no human hand can rival nature's paintbrush. The dramatic sunset in Joshua Tree National Park is a masterpiece of color in the California sky.

The cliffs of Colorado's Black Canyon of the Gunnison present a savage beauty as they plunge over 2,700 feet to the river below. The canyon is more than twice as deep as the Empire State Building is high. Pages 42–43: deciduous trees on the canyon floor form a green canopy to cool the fiery colors of Zion's sandstone cliffs.

Modeled on ancient Puebloan architecture and built of native stone, the Desert View watchtower guards the eastern edge of the Grand Canyon's South Rim, with panoramic views from sunrise to sunset.

White-tailed deer can bound at speeds of up to 40 miles per hour, even through thick forest terrain. When frightened or running, they hold their tails erect like a flag, revealing the distinctive white underside that gives them their name.

Gray wolves once ranged over much of North America, but are now an endangered species in the United States outside Alaska, numbering fewer than 2,500. Most live in Minnesota and neighboring states, with a few in the northern Rockies and northern Cascades.

Carlsbad Caverns in New Mexico is one of the largest cave systems in the world. Its magical calcite formations, from delicate soda straws to giant columns, have earned it World Heritage Site status. Opposite: like lone sentries, the sculpted sandstone buttes and mesas of Monument Valley rise dramatically out of the flat desert floor. These towering monoliths have become a symbol of the American West. Pages 48–49: blasted out of the granite rock of Mount Rushmore in South Dakota's Black Hills, this monumental sculpture of four presidents took 14 years to carve and was still not finished when the sculptor, Gutzon Borglum, passed away in 1941.

Unlike sandstone arches, natural bridges are formed by water. This is one of three such formations in Utah's Natural Bridges National Monument, formed by an ancient tributary of the Colorado River.

The Great Smoky Mountains are the highest in the eastern United States, and among the oldest in the country. Logging destroyed nearly two thirds of its hardwood forests, but they have revived since the Great Smoky Mountains became a national park in 1934.

The Everglades are often called a "river of grass," due to their vast expanse of sawgrass. The habitats vary from pinelands to mangroves to hardwood hammocks, and include indigenous plants found nowhere else.

Red foxes live in most parts of North America, but avoid deserts and dense forests. They are thought to be more numerous now than when Europeans first arrived in the 16th century.

The Gooseneck, seen from an overlook near the eastern border of Canyonlands National Park, shows the Colorado River at work, carving its way through the sedimentary sandstone of the Utah desert. Opposite: rivers, rain, and run-off from Mount Rainier's 27 glaciers rush down the slopes in impressive cascades such as Silver Falls. The mountain is an active volcano, yet covered in ice and snow. Pages 56–57: Death Valley marks the lowest point in the United States at Badwater, 282 feet below sea level. Only sand dunes and salt flats remain from the prehistoric lake which once filled this landscape.

The riverbed is the only path through the Narrows, a 16-mile trail in Zion National Park. It leads through Orderville Canyon, where the rock walls are 2,000 feet high, but at times only 20 feet apart.

The American pine marten is a small member of the weasel family, but unlike its cousins, it is able to climb trees. It lives in dense conifer and hardwood forests in the northern United States and Canada.

Few creatures evoke a sense of wilderness like the grizzly bear.
This threatened species now lives only in the northwestern states,
in Canada, and in Alaska.
Opposite: with a flurry of feathers and splashes, a group of birds takes
flight from the Everglades. The southern wetlands provide sanctuary,
feeding, and breeding grounds for hundreds of species.
Pages 62–63: the gorges of Utah's remote and barren Canyonlands
were gouged out by the Green and Colorado rivers. The confluence of
these two mighty rivers is a prominent feature in this national park.

The play of light and shadow on the rock formations of the Southwest casts an ever-changing mood over
the landscape. At Ribbon Arch, the fiery reds of midday give way to the somber muted pinks at sunset.
Opposite: you won't find any letters in the Devil's Postpile, only basalt columns up to 60 feet high, formed
around 100,000 years ago. This California national monument is set in pristine mountain scenery,
southeast of Yosemite.
Pages 66–67: seemingly endless vistas untouched by man are preserved for posterity in the national parks.
They offer us a chance to retreat, relax, and reflect on the nature of our existence.

A prickly pear cactus clings to life on a patch of earth in a rugged, rocky canyon. The tenacity of desert plants in such a harsh environment is a wonder of the Southwest.

Opposite: the South Kaibab Trail descends to the floor of the Grand Canyon through a majestic and ancient landscape of stone. Here, a human feels very small indeed.

Pages 70–71: the massive granite face of Half Dome, one of Yosemite's most famous peaks, towers 8,842 feet high, and is all the more formidable when blanketed by winter snow and ice.

Plumes of steam rise from a cinder cone on Kilauea, one of the most active volcanoes on earth. It is surrounded by the fascinating terrain of Hawaii Volcanoes National Park.

Opposite: a lone saguaro reaches toward the striated pink sky of an Arizona sunset in Tucson's Saguaro National Park. These majestic cacti can live for up to 200 years and reach heights of 50 feet, but their first "arms" don't appear until they are between 50 and 70 years old.

Pages 74–75: nature is a master sculptor. The striations in the deep-red cliffs of Navajo sandstone in Zion National Park were created over millions of years by the effects of erosion and the receding inland seas.

The desiccated trunk of a fallen tree spans a chasm in the limestone cliffs of Bryce Canyon. In contrast to the rocky vistas, Ponderosa pines, fir-spruce forests, and meadows border the rim of the plateau. Opposite: the 450-foot long Thurston lava tube was created by molten lava flowing through a cooled and set crust. It is one of the phenomenal features created by volcanoes on Hawaii's Big Island.

Set between high mountain glaciers and the rugged Pacific coast, Olympic National Park contains the world's largest temperate rainforest. The giant-sized trees are draped with vines and moss, while ferns blanket the forest floor.

A cast of whimsically named geologic characters inhabits the Devil's Garden in Arches National Park.
You can wander among the Three Gossips, Sheep Rock, and the Organ, or take a rest beneath the Tower
of Babel and Courthouse Towers.

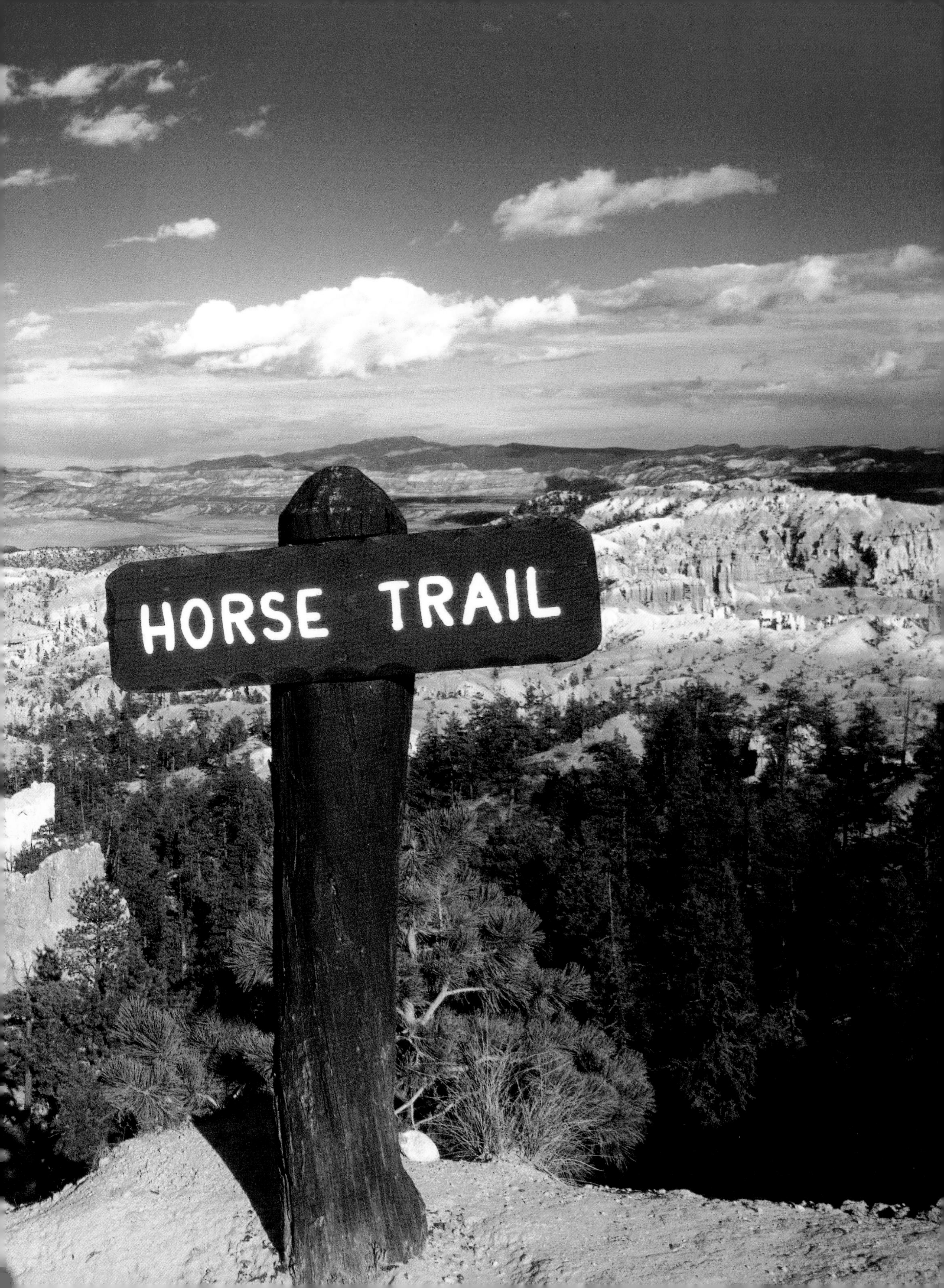
HORSE TRAIL

Bull elk are among the most majestic animals of the wild. Their mighty antlers, which can weigh up to
40 pounds per pair, grow every year, primarily to display dominance during the rutting season.
Opposite: the awesome beauty of Antelope Canyon is a spiritual experience, bringing people into harmony
with nature. It lies on Navajo tribal land, and for the elders, visiting here was like entering a cathedral.
Pages 82–83: numerous trails lead deep into the dreamlike world of Bryce Canyon. Those who don't want
to hoof it on their own two feet can wind their way among the cliffs on the back of a horse or mule.

*Fishing Cone geyser lies on the shore of Yellowstone Lake. In the early days of the park, visitors could
catch fish here and cook them by lowering their lines into the boiling water of the hot spring.
Opposite: look up in wonder at the ancient giants of Big Basin Redwoods State Park in California.
Only a few groves of these coastal redwoods, which reach heights of over 300 feet, still remain.*

Yellowstone is home to the only herd of free-roaming bison in the US. Once numbering in their millions, by 1890 these great beasts had been hunted almost to extinction. Today only 350,000 remain. Opposite: just north of San Francisco, Mount Tamalpais is a quick retreat from the urban landscape, with its waterfalls, lakes, rocky outcrops, redwood groves, oak woodlands, hiking and biking trails.

"Climb the mountains and get their good tidings. Nature's peace will flow into you as sunshine flows into trees," wrote the conservationist John Muir. He campaigned for the protection of his beloved Yosemite, which became a national park in 1890.

From its glacier-topped mountains through its lush rainforest to its wild Pacific coast, Washington's Olympic is three parks in one. Sea stacks and small islands and a host of marine life lie just offshore.

Gray foxes inhabit the deserts of the American Southwest, often making their dens in the rocky crevices of the canyons. They also live in wooded areas and are adept at climbing trees.

Opposite: a gnarled juniper clings to life in a world of stone in Arches National Park. In the background, Delicate Arch rises 45 feet high above the edge of a slickrock basin.

Pages 92–93: the Colorado River carved out the Grand Canyon, which is 277 miles long and up to 18 miles wide, over a period of 5 to 6 million years. The colorful walls of the sculpted buttes, bluffs, and mesas reveal nearly 2 billion years of the Earth's geological history.

INDEX

ACKNOWLEDGMENTS

The Automobile Association would like to thank the following photographers, companies and picture libraries for their assistance in the preparation of this book.

Abbreviations for the picture credits are as follows: - (t) top; (b) bottom; (l) left; (r) right; (AA) AA World Travel Library.
2t ©Medio Images/ImageState; 2c ©Getty Images/Photodisc; 2b ©Brand X/ImageState; 3 AA/M Van Vark; 4 ©Brand X/ImageState; 6 ©Medio Images/ImageState; 8 ©Brand X/ImageState; 9 ©Medio Images/ImageState; 10 ©Brand X/ImageState; 11 AA/ M Van Vark; 12 AA/L Provo; 13 ©Brand X/ImageState; 14 AA/ M Van Vark; 15 ©Getty Images/Photodisc; 16 ©Brand X/ImageState; 17 ©Medio Images/ImageState; 18 ©Medio Images/ImageState; 20 AA/M Van Vark; 21 AA/R Ireland; 22 ©Brand X/ImageState; 23 AA/R Ireland; 24 AA/Kirk Lee Aeder; 26 AA/ M Van Vark; 27 ©Getty Images/Photodisc; 28 AA/R Ireland; 30 ©Medio Images/ImageState; 31 AA/M Van Vark; 32 AA/D Lyons; 33 ©Brand X/ImageState; 34 AA/D Lyons; 36 AA/ M Van Vark; 37 Photodisc; 38 ©Medio Images/ImageState; 40 AA/M Van Vark; 41 ©Medio Images/ImageState; 42 AA/M Van Vark; 44 ©Brand X/ImageState; 45 AA/ M Van Vark; 46 ©Getty Images/Photodisc; 47 ©Getty Images/Photodisc; 48 ©Brand X/ImageState; 50 ©Brand X/ImageState; 51 ©Medio Images/ImageState; 52 ©Medio Images/ImageState; 53 ©Brand X/ImageState; 54 AA/J Tims; 55 ©Getty Images/Photodisc; 56 ©Brand X/ImageState; 58 ©Brand X/ImageState; 59 ©Brand X/ImageState; 60 ©Brand X/ImageState; 61 ©Getty Images/Photodisc; 62 AA/ M Van Vark; 64 ©Getty Images/Photodisc; 65 AA/J Davison; 66 ©Medio Images/ImageState; 68 ©Brand X/ImageState; 69 ©Brand X/ImageState; 70 ©Medio Images/ImageState; 72 AA/M Van Vark; 73 AA/M Van Vark; 74 AA/M Van Vark; 76 AA/Kirk Lee Aeder; 77 ©Brand X/ImageState; 78 AA/Kirk Lee Aeder; 79 AA/M Van Vark; 80 ©Brand X/ImageState; 81 ©Medio Images/ImageState; 82 AA/M Van Vark; 84 ©Medio Images/ImageState; 85 ©Getty Images/Photodisc; 86 ©Brand X/ImageState; 87 AA/K Paterson; 88 ©Medio Images/ImageState; 89 Photodisc; 90 ©Brand X/ImageState; 91 ©Brand X/ImageState; 92 AA/M Van Vark; 94 ©Getty Images/Photodisc; 95 AA/M Van Vark.

Every effort has been made to trace the copyright holders, and we apologise in advance for any accidental errors. We would be happy to apply the corrections in the following edition of this publication.